Preface

For a period of two months, in July and August 2006, a group of young Mennonites cycled across the United States, stopping in Mennonite communities to have conversations about the church. We rose early most mornings, cycled more than 85 miles per day, ate big meals together, met with churches whenever possible, and went to bed late – having discussions about our lives and the church all along the way.

The whole undertaking was an enormous one and came together very quickly. It was, in fact, less than three months from the initial brainstorming session in Elkhart, Ind., to the first day of biking into Portland, Ore.

We shaped our vision "on the road," conceptualizing and articulating our "mission *haiku*" as we climbed and descended the Rocky Mountains in southern Wyoming. We shared personal life stories with each other early on and these became central to effective communication within the group and to challenging each other in love.

And so we are grateful to Mennonite Mission Network for the opportunity to share a few of our stories with you in the pages to follow. It would, of course, be impossible to adequately represent the entirety of what happened to us in words … all the more so in the few words allotted to us in this small booklet. We will try, nonetheless, to offer a few glimpses into the joys and struggles, both collective and individual, that we experienced during our summer journey. Additional reflections can be found on our Web site – www.bikemovement.org – along with more pictures, statistics and general information.

BikeMovement participants – who were mostly white, middle class, university educated, young and Mennonite – chose to ride for a variety of reasons. For some, it was an adventure in camping, cycling and community. For others, it was an opportunity to think about church in old and new ways, both appreciative and critical. For still others, it was a chance – for once! – to be with young people who actually cared about the church, who were willing to give it "one last chance" as they struggled with their identity as a churchgoer, Mennonite or Christian.

In a sense, we were doing church out there on our bikes, sharing our stories and challenging one another in terms of Christian witness and discipleship, social responsibility, transparency, community, God-talk, and in many other areas. There were wonderful times of healing and joy … and terrible times of betrayal and pain. Church is not always exciting, worshipful or even a tolerable place to be – and neither are the deserts of southern Oregon in the month of July! But as individual members of God's people struggle collectively and continually to "dis-cover" the *missio Dei* – God's mission in the world – they begin to "re-member" the exciting, worshipful and irresistible aspects of church.

Interpretations of the BikeMovement experience are widely varied. What we lived together was a collective engagement in one another's stories as they emerged out of the context of the Mennonite Church. We learned to appreciate some of the diversity of the contemporary Mennonite experience, as well as some of the similarities and peculiarities that bind us together.

What we experienced as individual participants, however, cannot be summarized in a couple of sentences. And, unlike the collective sense of growth and learning that will likely remain a significant piece of BikeMovement USA 2006, our personal experiences were not generally so neatly packaged.

Indeed, some participants are still wondering whether last summer was hopeful at all. Our reflections on "church" ranged from the ways in which it can be extremely life-giving, to the times when we do not understand the significance of church at all. We as participants tried to ask ourselves the same questions that we used to facilitate conversations in the congregations we visited: "What has been your experience with church?" And, "What are your dreams for the church?"

Most of us in BikeMovement have had both good and bad experiences with church. But, more importantly, *all* of us have big dreams for what the church *could* be if it were to "fulfill its purpose," "be relevant" or "truly follow Christ."

A group of young Mennonites cycled across the country in the summer of 2006 because they had questions for the church. Some of those questions were positive and thankful. Others were critical, even angry. And many were a mixture of all these emotions combined.

But nearly all of the questions came from a sense of connectedness – whether "joyfully engaged" or "regretfully tied" – to the Mennonite Church. We rode more than 3,000 miles and had at least as many conversations, because we take church – and God's mission in the world – seriously. We invite you to join in the conversation as you read our reflections on the pages to follow.

Tim Showalter, Goshen College

BikeMovement
A Mennonite young adult perspective on church
Alicia Horst and Tim Showalter, editors

"Groovin' with the move...ment"
BikeMovement journal (August 20, 2006)
Anna Roeschley

I waved good-bye in my bare feet, down at the end of the drive, blowing kisses to the BikeMovement caravan as they rolled away into the distance, eastward bound. The bikers had departed earlier; I now remained, my toes wet with dew as I took slow strides up to the Nissley-Wenger's charming back porch – a haven for reflection until my ride arrived to take me back west. Light was still making its way into the sky, and church was going on next door.

I have an immediate sense that my trip is over. I have journeyed with these bikers for one week – one of the most challenging weeks of my life, on many levels. I have physically surpassed what I feared I could not do. I have been immersed in a uniquely intense communal experience. I have joined others in asking questions and engaging in dialogue that push what we know as the established church, that push what we know as established society, spirituality, and what it means to be in authentic community. I entered this journey with challenges, and I leave challenged.

Thus, my deeper sense is that this journey is not over; it is called a bike *movement*, not a bike *trip*. I am a part of this movement prior to, amidst and following these days on the road from Chicago to Columbiana. I believe this movement was happening even before the conversation took place last spring that pulled this group of people together and sent us biking. And this movement continues.

I am sad to part with these bikers only six days from the coast, especially after just starting to truly get in the BikeMovement groove.

I trust, however, that it docs carry on, that each of us is part of the overall movement and the movement a part of us. It is conversation, it is questioning, it is challenge. More than anything, it is community. Why do we do it? The questions threading throughout BikeMovement have been: What is church? What is community? But the questions I am left with this Sunday morning, with a worshiping body singing one way down the road and a biking community riding down the other, are these: Why do we engage in this wearisome seeking? Why do we ask those often painful questions and enter into such tense and tricky dialogue? Why do we do church? It is such a difficult endeavor. Why do we do this, work hard for something, some community, despite the tiresome effort it takes and the pain it involves and the brokenness? Why church? Vulnerability, relevance, openness, practicality – what does that mean? What does that look like? Is this kind of intentional, communal, life and faith journeying we envision really possible?

As I said, I leave challenged. I leave asking, questioning, seeking. I leave trusting that in this I am not alone, that the movement continues, that others are seeking and asking some of the very same questions. At a fundamental level, I think this is what a faith community might be about. At the very least, it is hope.

A dream for the church
Remembering faith amidst the glorious mess of post-modernity
Tim Showalter

Something about the BikeMovement experience made me revisit post-modernity. The word itself came up many times in our conversations. But there were other things – the most important being the group's frequent incapability to claim a truth (or, rather, a Truth in the absolute sense). This, on occasion, seemed to undermine much of the potential "helpfulness" of our conversations.

Post-modernity is by most definitions … indefinable, so I won't attempt to do so here. Were I to highlight some of its features, however, I would say this: Post-modernity suggests a transition from a period of Modernity, during which time the Enlightenment reached its apex and gave way to a global community ushering in a new way of seeing the world. Whereas the Modern world trusted science, progress and an essential quest for Truth that might explain the universe, the post-modern world is more satisfied with fewer ultimate answers, more willing to heed the advice of the past, and less inclined to call truths (with a small "t") "absolute" or "universal."

Our generation's general reluctance or inability to align ourselves with any particular capital "T" (Truth) is part of what makes intergenerational conversations so difficult in the church today. When Alyson, for example, travels to Vietnam and lives with a hospitable, caring and respectably religious Buddhist family, it is harder for her to say that Jesus is the "only way to heaven." And when Ebony hears convincing evidence for biological evolution in her pre-med courses, it is more difficult for her to stand in a tradition of strict Creationists.

The fear, of course, is that Alyson and Ebony will be "lost" to the world in their search. The reality most of the time, however, is that the Ebonys and the Alysons are longing for meaningful conversation based on deep faith commitments, placing them at odds with "the world." Without years of nurture and education in a community that holds Jesus as central and God's creation as a priceless blessing to humankind, Alyson and Ebony would not even be having these questions in the first place.

Modernity urged its children to respond to questions by looking for the practical "answer" that lies in the Truth. In cases like those of Alyson and Ebony, for example, Modern minds might have searched hard for the "right words" that would help to bring the two young rebels back to Christian faith, i.e., the Truth. Post-modernity, on the other hand, encourages its children to live within the tensions of their questions, recognizing that our small "truths" – the stories and experiences of our lives – will never get us to the Truth.

Post-modernity suggests that defining Truth in the here and now is not the point. Like those blind folks describing an elephant as they groped around touching its trunk, tail and sides, so we too can grasp more of the Truth only as we share our small truths.

For Ebony, getting to a place where she can say "Creationists are right and Evolutionists are wrong" is not the point of being a Christian. For her, following Jesus lies in the questions of discovery that probe the contradictions and intersections of her understanding of the creativity of God and the exploration of biological evolution. She is asking, "How can we hold creationism and evolutionary thought in dynamic, life-giving – and, yes, Christian! – tension?" As Ebony experiments, like Christians of old, with the relationship of the children of God to the world, it is *this* question that is central for her. It is *here* that she struggles with the age-old dilemma of exploring what it means to be "in the world, but not of it."

The danger is, of course, easy to identify. It is the slippery slope toward relativism. Post-modernity's critics are quick to argue that if we are limited in our considerations to others' experiences, then ultimately we can conclude nothing at all. For anything one says can always – and probably will – be discounted by someone else's experience. And, if such a philosophy dictates our thinking, don't we have to concede that David Koresh had a "small truth" of his own?

This, I believe, is where the church comes in. "Church" in Greek is *ekklesia*, which means a "gathering" or an "assembly." The Anabaptists considered church to be a body of believers gathered together to discern Truth. And the church in Acts 2 "had all things in common" and "spent much time together." God's people throughout the continuous story of faithful Christianity have struggled *in community* with their questions. As a church, as a gathered, believing community of faith, our calling is to hold each other accountable in our search for Truth. Individual questions remain pointed toward that ungraspable Truth only by the challenge of other individual questions. This is the power of communal discernment. I would argue that David Koresh's "truth" – his understandings of Christianity – would likely have been positively mitigated had he been engaged in discerning that truth within the context of a questioning community.

Christians are asked to live with one metaphorical foot in the kingdom of God and the other in "the world." Historically, Christians have always been, and still are today, in constant conversation about what that means pragmatically. Alyson and Ebony have questions about what it means to be a Christian in our contemporary world where Christians are studying evolutionary biology and living with Buddhists.

You as the reader of this booklet might have very different questions than those of Alyson and Ebony – questions that conflict in fundamental ways with their presuppositions. Faithful Christianity in the post-modern context asks not that you encourage Ebony or Alyson to believe what you believe, but that you engage their questions with your own. Perhaps then, through sincere, mutual engagement in our various truths, we will begin to more fully understand and enable ourselves to live within the complexities of God and the universe.

It is easy for us to say that we cannot fully understand God, but to enact that doctrine is another thing altogether. To live like we don't know who God is means accepting everyone's "truth" as signifiers of God's identity and, then, living within the tension of the questions that come out of holding those various truths in conversation.

As we learn to admit that our truths might not be the final Truth, and as we offer to others our small "t" truths, sincerely receiving their truths as equally significant experiences of Truth, we begin in a more holistic way to shape our lives around these various pieces of Truth and to grasp the overwhelmingly vast and complicated nature of God and God's creation.

A brief experience as a differently-abled person
Alicia Horst

I broke my right ankle early this summer while I was training for BikeMovement. I don't really know how I did it, but I do know that it hurt and that I was incapacitated for the next six weeks. The idea of training to ride a bicycle across the country was no longer remotely a possibility. I started walking three days before I flew out to Oregon for the beginning of BikeMovement. I was so happy to be able to walk again.

Making my way from one connecting flight to another on my way to Oregon for BikeMovement's launch was very painful. I tried to be careful and take it easy, but I soon realized that to keep up

I would just have to swallow the pain and keep moving. Even as an observer when the bikes touched the Pacific Ocean, on the day BikeMovement began, I had trouble walking up the large sand dune back to our campsite. And when we were in Boise, Idaho, my ankle was still stiff enough that I couldn't walk down stairs normally. I got used to my limp. When I witnessed Kendra hit the side of a vehicle in Wyoming, I found myself unable to run to her aid. The ankle simply required time and rest, both of which I felt I did not have.

My BikeMovement friends would often encourage me to think about riding. And I *did* think about. However, I was always struck by their pace. The group prided itself in talking through stats every day that explained how fast they had covered a certain amount of mileage. There was no way I would be able to keep up. Nathan and I were talking about my situation one day. He said, "I won't lie, I like to push myself. I don't like to go slow. But if you decide to ride, I'll ride with you."

So one day in Ohio, I rode a bit. Only 20 miles. For a once-again first-time rider, however, it felt like a decent distance. I was terrified of the bike, my imagination going wild with spectacular crashes and new phenomenally painful hidden broken bones. I rode slowly. *Very* slowly. And Nathan, Sarah and Jill stayed with me the whole way. After a few miles, Nathan said, "Let's pick it up a bit." So I started

riding a little faster, knowing that if something went awfully wrong again, three people were now with me.

This experience could have remained a personal accomplishment of sorts, one that pales in comparison to the thousands of miles traversed by many in the group. However, my awareness of what it felt like to be differently-abled over those months influenced the way I experienced hospitality in general. Whenever new persons joined our group, I was keenly aware of how our pace might be experienced by someone who was just beginning to ride.

I began to reflect on the ways that the church has and has not been a welcoming, hospitable community. What pace have we set?

What expectations do we have? Are we clearly articulating what we expect from people or do we assume they already know all there is to know about the church? What if people are never able to "measure up" to some standard of excellence that we have set for ourselves? Are our pace and productivity so important that we are willing to sacrifice relationships and a true experience of community? How do we learn to operate not out of a need to massage our own ego, but out of the context of caring for The Other among us? And what, in the end, is "us?" On what do we base our identity? Is this identity worth keeping?

Afterthoughts
Andrea Weaver

In the time that has lapsed from the final BikeMovement gathering, I have been continuously thinking about the significance of the BikeMovement journey. Every day my mind drifts back to those August days when a group of committed cyclists covered great lengths to interact with active listeners about the church. Writing this piece is my chance to reflect and process my BikeMovement experience. In an attempt to make sense out of the experience, I have two questions. First, why did I choose to participate in BikeMovement? And second, did I gain any deeper understanding about myself, the church or the world?

In order to tackle the first question, I need to say a word about the design of the bike journey itself. BikeMovement was an activity oriented toward interacting with the environment. The two spheres BikeMovement intentionally sought out were the *natural* and *church* environments. The transition from cycling/socializing in one environment to visiting/socializing in the other was very quick and sometimes quite abrupt. It seemed paradoxical at times to combine an institutional, tradition-governed and historical environment (church) with a free, physical-law-determined environment (natural). Even though the two environments were somewhat conflicting, one needed to have a strong interest in both of them to fully engage in BikeMovement. My own personal interest in both the "natural" and "church" environments is what attracted me to participate in the journey.

Now that I have described my choice to engage, what did I learn or gain through the experience of deeper understanding about myself, the church or the world? In order to  answer this question, I have found my fingers paging through one of my college textbooks, *Social and Cultural Anthropology* (New York: Oxford University Press, 2000). The authors, John Monaghan and Peter Just, wrote from their practices of ethnography. Each anthropologist invested time observing, participating and living in different cultural settings. The two then conversed about their independent experiences and collaborated to report on similar themes.

I was attracted to the following noted theme about belief systems: "It seems apparent that one thing religion of belief helps us do is deal with problems of human life that are significant, persistent and intolerable" (p. 124). This quotation surprisingly gave me insight into the way BikeMovement influenced my perception about myself, my church and the world. The insight I gained is best explained if I supplement the word "BikeMovement" for the phrase "religion of belief" in the above quotation. This then reads: "[BikeMovement allowed me] to deal with problems of human life that are significant, persistent and intolerable."

Let me be clear that I am not equating BikeMovement with a religion. I am simply describing how BikeMovement, like religion (or maybe the church), is a coping mechanism to deal with life-related anxieties. I found solace and peace in realizing that the internal questions I had regarding my association with the church were reciprocated by other individuals. My ability to see and experience how others wrestled with these questions gave me understanding into why people commune together. I think it is safe to generalize in saying that *all* BikeMovement members needed the other participants to share questions and thoughts.

BikeMovement was significant for me to understand the need to interact within different environments and to develop support networks. I am thankful for my chance to experience BikeMovement.

A bicyclist's prayer
(breathed in the rhythm of the road)

Holly Showalter

Oh God of winds and
storms prevailing,
Let not breath
and burn I've born
down in these
wheels be wasted but
infused, instead,
with spirit sent as
word and breath and
burning
for us in us so

that every drop of oil
I refuse to use may fuse
with every drop of sweat I pay
in dues and lose in hues
of love. And rage

(cause love gets angry harder,
    and also holds on longer.)

That they fall as tears
for slews of do's and
you'd-better-not's confusing
in a ruse of whose choosing?
Who is choosing?

(and also,
    who is asking?)

That we from faithful ones
in pews, worn shoes, and
bruised Chicago alleys take
the truths, the cues, the moves,
the rueful clinging to the least
(of these, we're no
    better, smarter, stronger.)

That love prevents our
hate-strewn views from making
refuse of once open hearts
while we peruse the news
each noon
and muse on how to soothe

(seeking more to do
    less to judge and complain.)

I've paid my dues
in miles and mountains
claimed my righteous blues
as SUVs cruise, bruising, by
I say, in interviews, to prove . . .

(but in the end
    must hand them over.)

That it be God who
glues and screws and smoothes
the loose ends and the loosened
which
includes each one of us who
though
keep trying fail to produce
but hues of dews

(that might have been rivers,
    are meant to be lakes and
    oceans.)

Bellwood hospitality

Holly Showalter

We rush in, brazen, talking, eating
me, at least, with sound idea
of what a Midwest, small-town
church's pastor, and his wife, too
are but find instead (oh laughing God)
no little understanding
tucked in giant generosity
of sojourney, exploration, stretching love
and (more unsettling still) of the
youthful passion I'd imagined we'd brought.

Chalupa lunches, sweet corn, tea,
in homes and churches, shops, wide open.
Act it out, then tell the stories
gathered later, 'round Sunday dinner
bowls of popcorn, plates of crackers.
It's the church what pulled them through
The hardest, deepest, profoundest times.
Community.
We saw, looking back, talking after
exactly what we came looking for,
asking and demanding
(in our brazen, youthen way)

Leaning

Holly Showalter

More often times than not
I'm scared of leaning too far over
Scared I'll get called a radical
Scared I'll get a cold shoulder
But leaning's what it takes
To get round curves with any speed
So leaning's what you learn to do
When momentum's what you need.

Becoming a community

Teresa Lehman

July 9, 2006, 11 people met together, some for the very first time, not knowing what to expect. In the weeks to follow, we were going to be spending more time together than most married couples do. We were going to be opening ourselves up to each other and become vulnerable.

My job on this trip was to do the grocery shopping, drive the car, and whatever else was needed. That meant that I was not able to spend as much time with the entire group as the bikers were able to do. Some lunches and dinners were difficult because everyone was continuing conversations that were started on the bikes. Everyone seemed to be getting to know each other and having great conversations with different people, but I was just in the background making sure everyone had enough food.

One of the important things that blurred this distinct separation was sharing our life stories. Each evening, when we were not meeting with an outside group, we would take turns sharing our life stories. Each participant opened up, making their life more transparent for the rest of the group. Speaking from my experience, this was very difficult because I am one to keep everything inside to avoid getting hurt by anyone. While sharing my story, I voiced some things to others for the first time. It was difficult, but at the same time, very freeing.

As each person shared, we were better able to understand where they were coming from. This process transformed us from 11 individuals into one community. The difficulties came when people started to leave the group and new participants joined. How do we as a community share what we had already shared, and then learn about new participants? As an original community, I believe we failed the different incoming participants. We were unable to find the time to continue the story-sharing process. I know that some of the participants felt like outsiders and had a difficult time fitting in and finding their place.

Now, if we are to relate this back to our church communities, what similar challenges do we face? Are we willing to open ourselves up and become transparent to the people that we live closest to and see on a daily basis? And if we get to that level of sharing, how do we then open up our community to welcome new people into the church or community? Returning from the summer's adventure, it is my desire to open myself to others, so that in turn they feel comfortable to open themselves up to me. This is a very difficult process for many, but I believe that God calls us to live in community.

Redefining church

Denver Steiner

At a lunch stop in Pennsylvania, a discussion broke out amongst the BikeMovement group as we were planning for that evening's church conversation. "I feel we've been misrepresenting what this trip is about," said one member. "We go into these churches, and people come away thinking that we are a group of young adults excited about saving the church. Well, I don't know if I even want to save the church." Others joined the discussion and, while our personal intentions in regard to church differed, most agreed that we had not been completely honest in the churches we had visited about how we felt as a group.

During that lunch discussion, I was reminded that each of us came from different church experiences and, therefore, had differing definitions of the word "church." Four weeks earlier, during a vision meeting in Idaho, I realized that each of us had very different reasons for joining BikeMovement. Despite our different goals and motives for the trip, we all agreed that we were seeking to create a meaningful place for open and honest dialogue to happen. Out of that meeting we penned our vision *haiku*: "Cultivating a relevant community through conversation." Looking back at my notes, I noticed I had written: "community = church ???"

Can we interchange community and church? Coming from a positive experience of church, I thought we could. After all, church should be a relevant community where honest conversation happens. However, I quickly learned from many of my peers that church hasn't been that for them. All of us had gone to church as kids, but to some, it had merely become a religious institution. Church members used "God" language in the Sunday meeting; however, the way they lived the rest of the week didn't always align with Christ's radical teachings.

Many BikeMovement members had discovered this hypocrisy after returning from a cross-cultural experience. They came home changed and filled with questions, but soon faced the reality of a home church that had not changed. When they did ask hard questions, their congregations did not know how to respond. Some were even told not to ask those questions!

Is this what Christ intended for His Church? I think we are missing the mark when church becomes a building where we meet on Sundays to be entertained by an overworked pastor. "Oh, but what about the relationships and potlucks?" you ask. While food and fellowship are indeed positive things, the danger is that church becomes a social scene for those who are biologically related or fit into the correct mold.

But even for the "in" crowd, what happens in this social scene can hardly be called conversation. At church, are we truly honest about our struggles and questions? Or are we really good at playing the church game and pretending that we have it all together? Despite our well-rehearsed biblical language on Sunday mornings, if we are not practically modeling what it means to walk in Christ's footsteps, then church is not a relevant place, especially for those who are earnestly seeking but do not fit into the social mold.

What are Christ's intentions for His Church? I believe Christ calls us to follow him. He does not intend for us to figure it out on our own. Church should be a community of believers who are discerning together what it means to be followers of Christ. The early church as described in Acts was a group of believers living this out. "All the believers were together and had everything in common. Selling their possessions and goods, they gave to anyone as he had need" (Acts 2:44-45 NIV). They believed this is what Christ meant when he commanded us to follow him. Church today should not be any different; it should be a way of living together, not a once-a-week social gathering.

Like my BikeMovement friend, I am not interested in saving church – if church remains defined as the dying social institution it has become today. My vision is to cultivate relevant communities where we struggle together, learn to love our neighbors, work for peace, take care of the world we live in, and learn together how to best live Christ's message in the 21st century.

A key step toward this vision is to begin having honest and open conversation with each other, especially with people who are very different from us. Intergenerational learning is important because we can learn what it means to be a follower of Christ from someone who has lived it and has faced similar questions. Intercultural learning is equally important because we get fresh perspectives into what it means to practically follow Christ within a context different from our own.

I wish I could call what I described above "church." But in order to do that, I think we need to examine traditional Sunday worship, and redefine church as a way of living together as a community of Christ seekers. We need to be open to new ways of doing "church" and think bigger than Sunday morning worship. In so doing, we can cultivate a relevant church community through conversation.

Know me

Kendra Nissley

"We don't know what to do
    with you!"
someone said.
You just don't fit.
No husbands or wives or kids,
you single young adults
drift
through the church:
Youthful, energetic,
passionate…
transient, awkward,
and Disillusioned.
With an insatiable desire for
adventure and the unknown,
you have nowhere, and
everywhere,
to go.
And so you slip through the
church's fingers, like sand.

We don't understand you,
we speak different languages,
constantly missing each other.
You've grown up in an era
when you can say, believe, do
Anything!
You're privileged!
The whole world is open to you,
and yet you can't seem to commit
to anything.
What is it that you want??

"We want relationships"
the young adults said.
We cry out with the desire
simply to know you
and be known by you: to be
recognized,
validated,
appreciated
for who we are
and not who we are wished to be,
nor the "future leaders" we
might
eventually
become.
Because we are leaders now!

"Know me"
is the cry of our, and every,
generation.
Listen to me,
but also hear me!!
Be vulnerable with me
as I am also vulnerable with you.
Answer my questions
with questions of your own
So that we might journey
together.
So that we might ultimately
know
Each other.

Indicates locations of church conversations and overnight stops

EVERY MONDAY
ALL ESPRESSO & CAPPUCCINOS $1.00

Deconstructing assumptions: learning to dream out of contextual relationships

David Landis

One theme that continually re-emerged in conversations during the bike journey was that relationships are at the core of meaningful encounters within a church environment. As I look back on our summer experience, these are some of the questions

that have been running through my mind: What does the central value of relationship mean for the future of the church? How does a post-modern culture interact with the value of relationships? How do these realities affect our creative ability to dream?

In working with Mennonite young adults throughout the past year, I have continually heard that my generation's connection to the church is different from those in the past. At age 24, I am a part of the first truly post-modern and Christian generation in the United States. Our world offers accessibility to a plethora of ideas, experiences and contexts that shape our worldviews theologically, philosophically and ethically. Within seconds, I can do a Google or Wikipedia search on anything and get a listing of other people's perspectives concerning my inquiry. Cheap airfares bring the world to my fingertips and allow me to personally explore my questions from a global viewpoint. Growing up with the privilege of accessible information offers a database of contextual understanding that helps me interpret the lives of persons around the world. Such a powerful tool makes life's decisions more complex, yet potentially more relevant to the world's needs.

By placing a high value on personal context, post-modern individuals can grasp relevant meaning in others' life experiences. Through a network of relationships, manifested values assimilated from individual life experiences can be the framework for a community's value system. As diverse people come together in community, the breadth of their experiences constitutes a bank of wisdom with which to serve the needs of today's world.

We often assume, however, that our context is shared by others. Such assumptions can serve to demonstrate our disregard for relationships and show people that we don't value them enough to learn from the wisdom of their experiences. We might further incorrectly believe that "what we need is what they need," and that the collective terms "us" and "them" are not connected. Assumptions of this nature promote an arrogance that narrows the potential for personal and community growth, stunting our ability to collectively imagine a better future into being. Assumptions, I believe, are a basic barrier both to understanding each other and to realizing our dreams.

We, of course, all approach our dreams with assumptions. But, based on our individual experiences alone, they inhibit our capacity to see the bigger picture. When gathered together in community, we need to find a space where these barriers to relationships can be articulated and deconstructed. Contextual relationship-building is crucial here, because without it, dreams formed within a community can only project in individual directions – a backfiring of the scope of their potential.

Through conversations on the bike journey, I heard a variety of assumptions based on the church's historic manifestation. I heard that structure is often more important than values. Security is more valuable than creative risk. The rigidity of religion will outlive movements. Sunday morning is more important than the rest of the week. Congregational membership is more highly valued than congregational diversity. Maintaining control is more hopeful than a dreamer's unstable landscape.

My vision for the church is that it will be able to continually recreate itself without the assumptions that are carried throughout history. We must seek a way where specific personal contexts do not become projected realities forced upon the entire community. We need to look beyond our personal experiences, our personal relationship with God, our personal relationship with the world, and begin to learn how the contexts of our communal relationships will affect our values and actions.

I often wondered on this journey if it is difficult for Mennonites to dream, and if our assumed religious parameters create this challenge. What might happen if we chose to craft a larger workspace from which to dream, from where our potential creative options might begin to expand? Contextual perspective does not exclusively promote either optimism or pessimism, so where will we go with the insight it gives us into our choices? We have the option to choose hope from these paths, or to choose those that are trailing off to destruction.

Conflict and the "circle process"
Anonymous

"We are just talking on two different levels!" Sharice snapped.

"I feel like you think every issue is a black-and-white issue, and it's exhausting," Jason challenged.

"Well, I have to go take a shower now, so whatever." Sharice stormed off.

After a hard day of riding through Oregon landscape in 90-degree heat, the BikeMovement members' physical bodies were not the only part of them at the point of exhaustion. From a conversation started on the road, Sharice and Jason were arguing about their personal experiences with racism and how that connected to the BikeMovement community, the broader church, and American society more generally.

While Jason and Sharice were engaged in the heated discussion, the rest of the 11-person team cleaned bicycles, prepared food, and took showers. Members periodically interjected a comment or two, reacted to a specific opinion with their body language, or attempted to avoid the conflict, pretending to take no notice of the conversation at all.

The poor end to the discussion and the tension in the air around the supper table that evening was alarming, as this was only the *fourth* day together as BikeMovement! Many people in the group came from a Mennonite legacy of conflict avoidance and suppression. A few members of the group recognized this history and called the group together with the intention of discussing the conflict.

The suggestion made was to use the "circle process." While such processes have historic roots in many societies for use in discussion and/or conflict resolution, most young adults today are not familiar with this practice.

Multiple methodologies are employed in circle processes, but all have three goals: (1) that everyone's voice is heard; (2) that respect is given for the careful processing of difficult issues; and (3) that working toward transformation of antagonistic relationships is a priority.

We sat in a circle as BikeMovement participants and shared how we had experienced the conversation earlier in the day. Each person was given the opportunity to say how they interpreted the snippets of the argument they had heard, why they chose to react to the conflict situation in the way they did, and how they felt about racism in their personal experience, in the church, or in the dynamics playing out among members of the biking team.

The circle process forced us to be honest about the conflict that had happened. It also helped us as a group to address an issue that was of great importance to the group – the desire to develop an understanding of what many young adults are experiencing in their relationships with the church, and how oppression and other barriers isolate them from others. The circle process was a helpful way to hold every member of the group accountable to engage in complex and difficult issues, and not to isolate Sharice and Jason in their discussion of such an important topic.

One suggestion that emerged from the circle process was that Jason and Sharice should have a second conversation a few days following the group encounter. The two agreed to do so, based on their commitment to the BikeMovement community and to their dedication to creating a climate where social justice prevails. In order to reduce the level of antagonism between the two of them and to facilitate a focus for the follow-up conversation, Jason and Sharice later agreed that a third party should be involved. They chose Veronica – a Bike-

Movement member, a gifted communicator, and the one who had served as facilitator of the circle process in the first place.

Jason and Sharice talked more gently in the follow-up conversation and left with a sense of respect for one another, recognizing how their critical thinking power, worldviews, passion, and different life experiences had shaped their perspectives on the matter. At one point in the encounter, Veronica asked Sharice and Jason to focus on how they experienced the conversation itself, rather than trying to figure out all the answers to the big topic of race issues.

Veronica explained that in the circle process, not only the initiative to discuss a hard issue is important, but just as crucial is the manner in which members talk to each other about it. Sharing with others about how the conversation feels (emotionally) can clarify that it is not a detached issue, even though it could be perceived that way (analytically).

Because of their different backgrounds and perspectives on race, racism and racial justice efforts, Sharice and Jason were unaware of how the other person experienced the issue. This unawareness had caused some of the most frustrating tension in the conversation because it whittled away at the trust and compassion between them. So although they might find themselves coming from somewhat different perspectives in the future, there was established in this encounter a sense of openness and safety to speak one's mind and ask the hard questions.

The dissolution of tension using the circle process was a new experience for some of us in the group. It was one example of how we might utilize methods of nonviolent communication, an essential value to community. It contributed to discussions about important topics such as honesty, community building, exclusion, oppression, accountability, love, etc. This circle process is just one example of the ways young adults in the Mennonite church can learn about what it means to be a community of seekers together, developing our values through conversation and doing theology in community.

A place for everyone

Bekah Moyer

Right now, the ten days I spent pedaling and riding in the support vehicle through the cornfields of the American Midwest this summer seem far removed. My head is filled with other things. When I do take the time to reflect, however, what sticks out most in my mind is the people – the people who were traveling with me, the people we passed by, and the people who touched the journey.

North Americans, both Christians and not, continue to amaze me. Just when I think they are selfish, egocentric, and competition-driven, they do something that amazes me. From the police officer at the airport whose question, "How can I help you?" when we were parked in a loading zone, to the woman who followed us in her car through a lightning storm, to the little girl who cried and held me tight when I left her home after an overnight stay, the people we encountered exhibited such empathy, altruism and love that I feel touched by God's grace to have them in my memory.

Perhaps it is simply the American sense to help an adventurer, but I think it is more of a tribute to humanity as a whole. BikeMovement is certainly not the first time I have encountered what could be called hospitality, but this experience was particularly filled with examples of it lived out.

There are many stories the group could tell of how we helped each other make the journey. I am a completely inexperienced biker and, on my third day with the group, I decided to try to bike. I managed to go 54 miles before lunch, but only because of some fellow bikers hanging back with me and cheering me on. When I finally rolled into our lunch site after literally whimpering up the last three hills, I felt largely like a failure. I looked at this group who had just done the same amount of biking and they seemed so at ease and energized, whereas I was exhausted, uncomfortable, and feeling guilty for slowing them down. I finished the day, thankfully, in the support vehicle.

It was the next day, which turned out to be a particularly hard ride, when Kendra said to me that I had inspired her to get through the day. "What?!?!" I thought. Here was Kendra who biked all the way from Oregon telling me that I inspired her! She said that what I had done the day before, with basically no biking experience, inspired and motivated her to keep going.

Slowly I learned through the ten days I traveled with the group that there is a place for everyone in a community, in the body of Christ, and how to be content with that. I want to be good at and able to do everything. That is my nature. When faced with something I may really just not be capable of doing, I make myself do it anyway. Through this biking experience, however, I have learned that to be part of a community and the church does not mean that I have to do everything or be everything myself. A true community, and real church, is a group that meets people where they are and grants them the grace and hospitality to work through their struggles and life journeys. We may not always have been that to each other on this trip, but sufficient examples abound to have proven it true.

I believe that young adults, and the church community as a whole, should take note and learn a little grace. For the church to travel with young adults through the journey and for young adults to have the grace to accept the church as it is – all the while looking to make it better – are lessons from this experience that should be taken to heart.

Naming ourselves

Kendra Nissley

I remember reading a blog entry in April about what later became the BikeMovement Web site, that announced in bold type: "We need to figure out a name for the project." BikeMovement was already an idea, the route was already being mapped out, and a number of people had already committed to the trip that would commence in three months … but it had not yet been named.

Many months hence, BikeMovement has become our official title, and over that time, the name has seen quite a bit of usage. "BikeMovement dot org!" Sarah Thompson would often call out to motorists who had their windows down at traffic lights. BikeMovement posters appeared in most of the churches where we stayed along the way, and we would often introduce ourselves with this title in the congregational conversations. Most of us carried business cards with "BikeMovement" in attractive letters on the front – cards that we handed out to any random stranger who showed even the slightest bit of interest in our journey. Some of the cards even showed up on bulletin boards – at one car wash in Des Moines, Iowa, and on a road sign somewhere in Nebraska – as if to announce to people we never met that "BikeMovement was here."

By now, it is safe to say that BikeMovement has become an important part of our identity, even though it started out as an idea without a name. Due to the nature of the experience, it is also an identity that can exclude anyone who didn't take part. That is only natural, you might say, and can be expected. How else can one hold together as a group if the members do not have an exclusive, shared identity?

This question was often raised in churches across America: "If we do not exclude certain people, how can we claim to be a distinctive community at all?" But where does one draw the line? And what of the people who have the misfortune of falling outside that line, of not feeling welcomed in our church community – the underdressed, the homeless, people leading lifestyles we might not approve of, non-Mennonites, young adults with crazy, impractical (and maybe slightly heretical!) ideas, non-Christians, etc.? Such people may go by different names, but collectively they are known as "The Other." And more often than not, they are not  welcome because *they* are different from *us* and they threaten *our* identity by *their* differences.

Before parting ways on August 26, 2006, those of us who finished the trip agreed that, if anyone else wanted to subscribe to our identity – bike around town, talk about stuff, and call themselves BikeMovement – they were allowed. Choosing not to feel threatened by "those people," we decided, without even knowing them, that they were welcome to be "one of us." Thus, we broke through the barrier, the backslash between "us\them," and made the difference obsolete. They were now us, and we, they.

Can the distinctiveness of Christianity also be defined by the commitment not to exclude anyone? By opening our arms to everyone? By practicing inclusive, accepting love in all relationships? Is this what Jesus would do? Isn't this what he *did*?

a flame in the ocean

Kristen Swartley

Absolutely unmixed attention is prayer. - Simone Weil

mostly i am leaves scattered
and burning from the flames
of too much and too much.
but there was

red amidst the waves,
a barn striking steady in the ocean
of swaying stalks.

one bike and one backpack,
one road at a time,
my legs pumping will carry
these questions:

take me speaking words.
i am a young western woman.
take me word.

i cannot be because i am not,
because i am losing knowing,
becoming forward and back-
ward everyday.

can i be what i have not seen?
can i live
what does not yet exist:

a way of eating, singing,
running that is right
relationships,
that is neither

female nor male,
stuck nor flurrying,
brown nor peach?

Come see the global church!
Excerpts from speech given at Hesston College/Anabaptist
Vision and Discipleship Series (October 27, 2006)

Sarah Thompson

Dreams are associated with fantasy, with intangibility. We dream only when we are asleep, or in a lapse of consciousness during the day. However, we dream in images that are recognizable. So if we are only exposed to certain shapes and colors, only those elements will comprise our dreams. In a similar way for the church, if we only know about a few ways of living as followers of Jesus, then we can only envision the church in this limited manner. I invite you into interaction with the global Anabaptist community, to add new colors, shapes and ideas to your design of the church of our dreams.

At this point in our history as an Anabaptist church, we are many churches around the globe. Twenty-five percent of the global Anabaptist churches are located in North America and Europe (the Global North). Seventy-five percent are in Asia, Africa and Latin America (the Global South). The 25 percent of the churches in the Global North own 95 percent of the total resources of this global church.

The global Anabaptist family gathers every seven years. We exchange ideas, enjoy one another's company, and most importantly worship God together – in times of joy and in times of suffering. I invite you to come see the church around the world, the people we call brothers and sisters in faith. The Global Youth Summit, which occurs two days before and then blends into the larger Mennonite World Conference, was created in 2003 in response to a growing articulation about the need for a specific space for young adults, simultaneous with integration into the larger body of the church.

At the summit, one wing of discussion covers contemporary issues that affect the youth and young adults in respective local contexts, and aid one another in discernment. For example, as the Mennonite Brethren in Canada just began to allow women in the senior pastorate, representatives from Paraguay will talk about the lack of gender diversity in their senior leadership (although they do love to mention that the First Lady of Paraguay is a Mennonite!). After growing up thinking that Mennonites did not dance, I learned at the summit that many Mennonites around the world, in fact, do dance and integrate movement into their worship.

The exchange of ideas and support strengthens the awareness of our interdependence and broadens conversations and visions for the church. This summer the BikeMovement community exchanged ideas with numerous people across the United States. The conversation at the youth summit, however, is a global conversation. In order to have a conversation of global proportions, the globe needs to be able to be there! The dynamics of the aforementioned unequal access to resources affect if and how we can meet to share. In recognition of this, we in the BikeMovement have contributed to the worldwide effort to raise $100,000 to build the capacity of the travel funds so that emerging young adult leaders from the Global South can participate in the upcoming 2009 summit.

The imperative to learn about one another is a foundational part of the church of my dreams. If this is all happening already, do I not have any criticisms or questions, or see challenges in the days ahead? Well, I do, and I hope you do as well. But at the same time I ask – no, I implore – you to come see the global church, that you may dream in more colors, that you may ask questions in more languages, that you might see and feel the encouragement of youth dedicated to what is required of us: to do justice, love mercy, and walk humbly with MotherFather God.

[**Editor's note:** Sarah Thompson is the North American representative to the Global Youth Summit of Mennonite World Conference. The next large gathering of the Anabaptist family will be held in Paraguay, July 13-19, 2009. Contributions to the young adult travel fund can be directed through MWC. Write "BikeMovement" in the memo line of checks.]

Embodied evangelism

Timothy H. Shenk

As we rode up to a stoplight in a small town in Ohio, a car driver rolled down his window and inquired about our biking. One group member quickly explained BikeMovement and then excitedly exclaimed, "You should come ride with us!"

I was struck by the ease with which we shared our story and invited a stranger to participate in the adventure. Were we street evangelists?

Across the country we consistently found people curious and interested in BikeMovement, whether they simply asked, "Where are you going?" or inquired more deeply about our combination of biking and church.

In the conversation at Hyde Park in Boise, Idaho, someone commented that coming into a church is a scary position to be in; the challenge is for the congregation to put itself in a position of vulnerability so that a stranger feels especially honored. Bicycling across the country is a vulnerable endeavor as well – slow pace, uncertainties, danger, exposure to weather conditions, willingness to try new things, needing help and hospitality, and being physically exhausted. Perhaps this is why we could "evangelize" in a nonthreatening, invitational way. We had something worth sharing.

We talked with many people who would ordinarily feel cautious about inviting friends or strangers to their church gathering. Do our gatherings truly demonstrate the abundant life that Jesus offers? Why do I see a disconnection between church as we know it and faithful discipleship to Jesus Christ?

One evening just before a conversation at a Mennonite church in Pennsylvania, I had the overwhelming need to leave the basement of the church building. I went outside near a graveyard, lay face down in the grass and cried. Later, I wrote in my journal: "How can we be prophetic [to the world and to the church]? I feel like crying as I see more and more clearly what it will mean to be prophetic. It will shake my life. People will hate me. People will love me. I can't handle either of those on my own."

The prophets cried out, "My soul is in anguish. How long, O Lord, how long?" Jesus cried, "O unbelieving and perverse generation, how long shall I put up with you?" During BikeMovement I cried a lot – both out of incredible joy and thanksgiving, and also out of extreme frustration and heartache. The Christ-centered church should be crying as we see the pain of the world, the suffering of our brothers and sisters, and as we witness the acts of beautiful transformation and hope. Let us embody the tears by becoming the space where "justice rolls down like water, and righteousness like a flowing stream."

Contributors

Dave Landis, 25, Harleysville, Pa. Graduated in 2004 from Eastern Mennonite University (EMU) with a major in Biology. Travel includes one semester in the Middle East and a 14-month round-the-world trip (see: vivaelviaje.com). Drawn to BikeMovement "to create a space for church communities and young adults to converse about their experiences with church." Currently working part-time for Franconia Mennonite Conference (Souderton, Pa.) in Web site development and young adult leadership cultivation. Will move to Jerusalem in fall 2007 to take graduate classes and to travel.

Teresa Lehman, 26, Chambersburg, Pa. 2004 graduate of EMU (Elementary Education). Private school second grade teacher before joining BikeMovement. Became interested after "hearing some conversations and struggles young adults are having in their spiritual and personal lives." Currently a substitute teacher in local schools, and Junior Youth leader and Sunday school teacher at Cedar Grove Mennonite.

Janet Rebekah Moyer, 26, Harleysville, Pa. Graduated from Bluffton University (2003) with BA in Fine Arts and Apparel/Textiles. Joined BikeMovement because "I was interested in the concept, in finding out what people are thinking, to get to know the people who participated, and to see some of this country that I have never seen before." Currently assistant manager at the Ten Thousand Villages store in Souderton, Pa.

Kendra Nissley, 22, Columbiana, Ohio. EMU grad (2007) in Justice Peace & Conflict Studies (JPCS) and German. Drawn to BikeMovement for the biking, and as "a potential safe space to express my worries, thoughts and questions." Presently completing an internship with the Summer Peacebuilding Institute (EMU), followed by a short, solo bike trip.

Anna Roeschley, 22, Flanagan, Ill. Graduate of Bluffton University (2007) with concentrations in Communication in Church Organizations and Peace and Conflict Studies. Drawn to BikeMovement because of "a sense of shared vision and the kinds of questions it was asking about church." Enjoys biking and had been desiring to complete a long distance bike ride. "BikeMovement seemed like a fitting community with whom to join and journey." Preparing for a period of service/internship in the fall.

Holly Showalter, Harrisonburg, Va. Following graduation from EMU (2004), served three years in Sichuan (China) as a teacher with Mennonite Partners in China. Especially loved BikeMovement for opportunity to "peek into different U.S. congregations and talk to others not wholly content in their church realities."

Andrea Weaver, 22, Perkiomenville, Pa. Home congregation, Salford Mennonite, hosted BikeMovement toward the end of the trip. Presently in first year of Master of Science program in Occupational Therapy at Thomas Jefferson University (Philadelphia). From BikeMovement, "gained insight about community living and group dynamics – very useful for my studies inside the occupational therapy domain."

Timothy Holsinger Shenk, 22, Harrisonburg, Va. EMU graduate (2007) with Liberal Arts (major) and Bible & Religion, Psychology, and History (minors). Drawn to BikeMovement to "seek first the kingdom of God" with a group of others on an adventure of faith. Loves kids and plans to work as gym teacher and assistant coach, living with wife, Cheryl, in Camden, N.J., in partnership with a Christian intentional community connected with Sacred Heart Church "in a neighborhood hurt by pollution and poverty."

Denver Steiner, 25, Orrville, Ohio. EMU graduate (2004) in Communication. Since then, working in marketing for a family tractor business that has "given me the flexibility to do video and Web design work on the side." One such project, an eight-month stint with Mennonite Media on documentary, *Shadow Voices*. As a child, lived five years in Bolivia, an experience that "sparked my love for travel and meeting people." Has given leadership to producing DVD documentary, *BikeMovement: A young adult perspective on church* (2007).

BikeMovement facts and stats

BikeMovement riders:

- Traveled for nearly two months, from July 10 to August 26, 2006.

- Covered a total of 3,580 miles.

- Clocked a collective 30,468 miles.

- Rode at an average speed of 15 mph.

- Started their journey in Tillamook (Portland), Ore., and ended in Ocean City, N.J.

- Ate more than 129 pounds of bananas.

- Facilitated about 20 conversations en route.

- Stayed in churches when they had connections and camped when they did not.

- Had as many as 16 riders on the day with the highest number, and as few as four on the lowest.

- Welcomed more than 60 riders who participated in at least one day of the journey.

- Required that each participant provide funds for their own personal food and bike/replacement parts.

- Gratefully received sponsorship in areas such as support vehicle gas and repair, bicycle parts, emergency needs, moral support, publicity, etc., from Franconia Mennonite Conference, Virginia Mennonite Conference, Eastern Mennonite Seminary, Virginia Mennonite Board of Missions, East Coast Bicycle Academy (Harrisonburg, Va.), and many other caring individuals.

- Released a DVD documentary about their experiences, entitled *BikeMovement: A young adult perspective on church* (2007). Ordering information can be found at www.BikeMovement.org.

Questions for reflection and discussion

1 What event or adventure in your lifetime comes closest to that experienced by the BikeMovement participants in the summer of 2006?

2 How did you find yourself reacting as you read this booklet? Were you thinking: "These guys are crazy!" or "I could never do that!" or "Sometime I would *really* like to participate in an experience like this!"

3 With which of the written pieces found here (essays, poems, journal entries, etc.) did you most connect?

4 What were some of the reoccurring themes that you noticed emerging as the BikeMovement participants reflected on their experiences?

5 Much is said in these pages about the relationship between "church" and "community." In your mind, how are these two realities similar or overlapping? How are they distinct?

6 In what settings or contexts have you felt comfortable voicing your most troubling questions about faith and the church?

7 How does the post-modern affirmation of the *individual* affect our understanding of church as a *community of people* with shared beliefs and commitments?

8 What, for you, have been the key elements of community that most foster meaningful relationships, hope, and a sense of the presence of God?

9 Has church, in your experience, been relevant in terms of engaging the needs of your local community and the world? In what specific ways has this been so? In what areas could the church improve?

10 The relatively young age of these writers brings up the question of generational perspective. How might the questions raised in this booklet be shaped by age and experience? And in what ways do the questions transcend generations?

For further reading

■ ARMSTRONG, Karen, *The Battle for God: Fundamentalism in Judaism, Christianity and Islam* (New York: Ballantine Books, 2001).

■ BROWN, Hubert, *Black and Mennonite* (New York: Sheed and Ward, 1969).

■ CAPUTO, John D., *Deconstruction in a Nutshell: A Conversation with Jacques Derrida* (Bronx: Fordham University Press, 1996).

■ CLAIBORNE, Shane, *Irresistible Revolution: Living as an Ordinary Radical* (Grand Rapids, Mich.: Zondervan Publishing House, 2006).

■ GANDHI, Mahatma, with JACK, Homer A., *The Gandhi Reader: A Sourcebook of His Life and Writings* (New York: Grove Press, rev. ed., 1995).

■ LEDERACH, John Paul, *Moral Imagination* (New York: Oxford University Press, 2005).

■ PRANIS, Kay, *The Little Book of Circle Processes: A New/Old Approach to Peacemaking* [in *The Little Books of Justice and Peacebuilding Series*] (Intercourse, Pa.: Good Books, 2005).

■ RODRIGUEZ, Jeanette, and Fr. VIRGILIO, Elizondo, *Our Lady of Guadalupe: Faith and Empowerment among Mexican-American Women* (Austin: University of Texas Press, 1994).

■ SIDER, Ron, *Rich Christians in an Age of Hunger: Moving from Affluence to Generosity* (Nashville: W Publishing Group, latest ed., 1997).

■ WEIL, Simone, *Waiting for God* (New York: Harper Perennial Modern Classics, 2001).

■ WIDJAJA, Paulus, KREIDER, Alan, and KREIDER, Eleanor, *A Culture of Peace: God's Vision for the Church* (Intercourse, Pa.: Good Books, 2005).

■ For additional young adult perspectives, see earlier issues in the *Missio Dei* series: *Students Talk about Service* (No. 7), edited by James R. Krabill and Stuart W. Showalter (2004); and *What I Learned from the African Church: Twenty-Two Students Reflect on a Life-Changing Experience* (No. 11), edited by James R. Krabill (2006).